Michael John Carignan has published several individual poems in literary magazines and newspapers. He published his first collection, *Chrysalis*, with Austin Macauley Publishers in 2021. The author's second collection, *Free Admission to My Mind*, is a deeper collection comprising many new poems. Mike started writing poetry in 1975 in high school. He graduated from Keene State College in 1979 majoring in psychology with a minor in both film and art. He recently began dabbing into standup comedy already going on stage twice in recent months.

This collection is dedicated to a number of people who never wavered in their faith in me. My girlfriend, Roslyn, always held an attentive ear while reciting my work to her and provided eager encouragement. Our friend Janet, who always has our backs and advice. My cousin Brian who inspired me with his knowledge working at a college library. My cousin, Jeff—our bond growing up always is there for me. And to Paul Doucette who produced a wealth of knowledge of the history of my hometown and the train that used to cross the rails near my house. My three sons are also never far from my heart.

Michael John Carignan

FREE ADMISSION TO MY MIND

AUSTIN MACAULEY PUBLISHERS®

LONDON • CAMBRIDGE • NEW YORK • SHARJAH

Ordering Information
Quantity sales: Special discounts are available on quantity purchases by corporations, associations, and others. For details, contact the publisher at the address below.

Publisher's Cataloging-in-Publication data
Carignan, Michael John
Free Admission to My Mind

ISBN 9798891552944 (Paperback)
ISBN 9798891552951 (ePub e-book)

Library of Congress Control Number: 2024918166

www.austinmacauley.com/us

First Published 2024
Austin Macauley Publishers LLC
40 Wall Street, 33rd Floor, Suite 3302
New York, NY 10005
USA

mail-usa@austinmacauley.com
+1 (646) 5125767

20241122

My brother Tim and I traversed the bridge, crossing the two-by-fours while my cousin Jeff looked on. We were about ten feet above the Merrimack River. We thought we were immortal, as a passing freight train would have easily shaken us enough to plummet into the river down below.

In the parlor of–
The mind's eyes–
Many guests come–
To visit for a drop or two–
Of advice or just ramble
On like a spiraling out
Of control train–
The room has a fragrance–
Of old familiar ways–
Although some of–
The darkest thoughts–
Leave muddy prints–
Along the way–
While others beam–
Like filtered light–
Bringing out the–
Best prizes of memory–
That will always have–
A place to stay–
This place is never locked–
No key was ever made.

The girls' camp now–
Long forgone–
A young boy donned–
His adolescent gloves–
Learned to mingle–
With other guys–
Around his age–
Taking canoes out–
To blueberry island–
Before the season began–
It was a celebration–
Of independence–
Before long hours–
In the kitchen–
Took their toll–
A pretty Mexican girl–
Danced with him–
Like the wind–
Exhilaration gained–
A smile of an evening–
That captured its own virtues–
Deep within.

People busy as bees–
Constructing their ways–
Refurbishing their sighs–
To ascend their ladders–
Of success–
Blinded by the–
Little accomplishments–
Left behind on the–
Gathering steps–
That claim occasional–
Profound meanings–
Like the clearing of–
The throat of a storm–
Before lightning illuminates–
The revelations forthcoming–
In the teardrop of a day–
As the queen rules the hive–
Our hearts really have–
The final say.

Sweet smell of jasmine–
Journeys through the air–
Bouncing off sidewalk cracks–
As it nestles in our hair–
Mid-august is a reminder
That soon the monarch cocoon–
Will cling to a shy branch–
Or dying leaf–
Before transforming–
Into the splendor–
That will be–
Fluttering off their thrones–
Of quiet boughs–
To the wonder–
Of the pastel skies–
Complimenting another hue–
From an unseen brush–
Of a heaven to behold–
So quickly is their death.

Sun baked rocks bathing–
In the turbulent stream–
Winked back jets of light–
Like history rising from–
The aftermath of thought
Hinting at what lies below
Thrashing to the surface
Now and then for air–
As the flourishing trees–
Spread their verdant hair–
Silent spectators looking on–
While a fallen leaf–
Backstrokes downstream.

Normalcy went to–
The clothes store for–
A new suit – someone whispered–
Take the loudest and brightest–
Off the rack as the tailor–
Was society and standards–
Change on a dime–
So adjustments will have–
To be continuously be–
Done even though–
Many people won't approve–
Take the loudest and brightest–
Off the rack–
With matching shoes–
To stroll out of any door–
You like.

Freshly caught nocturnal vision–
Brought on the scene–
To be examined post haste–
Before awakening as memory–
Evaporates from the slumber–
What transpired in the mind before–
Like a humming bird darting–
From the petals of a flower–
For only a split second–
It exists to vanish–
In thin air.

Tranquil those hot afternoons–
At long beach as we called it–
Opposed to short beach at–
The other end of the lake–
Swimming out to the first raft–
As the brave ventured out to–
The second resting on deeper waters–
Never pondering when we became immortal–
No way of drowning at adolescence height–
Finding out later that a young friend at 14–
Decided to be a would-be a seal to–
Traverse the three miles between–
Short beach and long beach in–
The dead of night after intoxication–
Straddled his back with each stroke–
Taken as destiny hog tied him–
To the end of his immortal ride–
To reach franklin shores with–
A breath to survive–
The hazy mist below swirled–
Like lazy dancers on a stage–
No one could abide–
Bubbles no one could describe.

Standing in youth–
Near my buddy's barn–
Dusk dominated the horizon–
As a single bat swooshed out–
From barely hinged door–
Feeling both fear and awe–
At this being flapping in–
The misty air–
Once a giant of my–
Domain with control–
At my adolescent reins–
It was so simple to lose–
All that was taken for granted–
With such movement of a breeze
A black figure released in freedom–
Upon the New Hampshire land–
A specter of grandeur–
For all to see–
A shadow with–
Its own inscription–
Upon the land.

Early morn sandy beach York–
Strolling down from cottage–
Before sons and soon to be–
Divorced wives make their way down–
Setting up blanket, cooler and umbrella–
Like Columbus claiming the new world–
As the sea gulls cawed looking–
For scraps – the metal detector people–
Violating the beach in hopes–
Of new treasures–
Discovering an empty bench–
With the ocean for my view–
Armed with a hot cup of java–
Wrestling with the thoughts–
Emerging for the new day–
As the waves ranked in–
Deep blues and greens–
Told ready made fortunes–
As sea shells lay abandoned–
For people to explore–
Serenity before –
The crowd of voices–
Intruded thoughts like–
An under-tow devouring everything–
In its way.

Following a ribbon of blue–
in my nautical twenties–
Donning the naval uniform–
In Japan – street closed off–
As cherry blossoms sang–
Their melodies on a warm day–
Native youth dressed up–
With greased back hair–
Marlboros rolled up in–
The boys' white T-shirts–
Girls with their poodle skirts–
Adorned with pigtails–
As a boom box vibrated–
Elvis Presley – drawing their enthusiasm–
People emulating another land–
Far from distant shore–
A wonder to see–
People in such harmony.

Back in the early days–
We called it Woodslake–
A dead end called Charles St.–
A boulder like entry with–
Our names painted on–
Marking our turf–
We met to share ourselves–
Cousins together with secrets–
A murmuring stream nearby–
My cousin and I explored a house–
Wounded by fire – a family gone–
The table set for supper – clothes on the line–
A pickle jar yellowed by time caught in–
A mason jar on the table–
As if death took a holiday for now–
Youth stenciled in memories–
Now a condo unit tarred over–
From the throes of yesterday.

The blue loon floated–
On the pond's surface–
Being quite an enigma–
Her shrill cry bounced–
Off the water's edge–
Nature at the best–
Like a dream risen
From the early fog
Bringing splendor–
For a short time–
Before she lifts–
Her huge wings–
And is gone.

Keep your smile–
Unlike the American dollar–
It will never devalue–
Only gain the self-worth–
Of others around you–
Like the kid in yellow slicker–
And galoshes finding–
Enjoyment in splashing–
In a new found puddle.

Sublet the apartment–
Of my mind–
Let others in–
To move their furniture–
In spaces that govern time–
Of things challenging–
The feelings of a man–
Whose will can at moments–
Waiver like an insect caught–
In a web – metamorphosing–
Into something completely different–
A new room added in–
A cerebral house seems so solid–
On lookers peering in–
The structure built from within–
With no for sale sign–
Gyrating in the wind–
With a cellar cramped–
With the past shut tight–
In hope chests labeled–
Yesterday.

Two shadows wearing elongated forms–
Practicing their chameleon states–
Struggle on a cerebral mat–
One wearing the crown of–
Repression – an interloper desiring–
To dominate the other called–
True expression many times–
Shunned by others who judge–
Where their own opinion gravitates–
But exposed in the harshest of light–
Two shadows wrestle in their–
Own race two vapor figures–
With society to keep pace–
In empty corners where–
Empathy no longer waits–
A birth of the blending–
Of the two – a delivery–
Resounding in the reality–
Of many shapes–
A clash in mortality–
That is every one's fate.

When in the kid stage–
There was a forgotten cemetery–
Along a long dirt path
In my home town of franklin–
Its residents all were–
A century or two old–
The headstones marking–
Their lives were either–
Tumbled over or crumbling–
From the ravages of time–
It was a moment to pay–
Tribute to these people–
As the tall grass attempted–
To cover up their demise.

In the cloak of night–
You are my candle —
Burning bright–
With tallow running down–
Like tears of joy–
To chase the shadows away–
You are the guardian of–
What comes right–
With colors like–
The flames twisting–
Upon the wick–
Our love abounds–
As all that seems–
So crazy is extinguished–
Again and again–
Like the candle–
With its cover–
Screwed on tight.

Tribute to Roslyn

The church clock awkwardly–
Inched its mammoth hands —
Forward – against a glass face–
In old franklin town–
As the Merrimack River–
Lazily rolled on its course–
Where Daniel webster took–
His last breath–
Like the train that stopped–
Roaring along the tracks–
Many years ago as–
A boy envisioning it all–
Lay deep upon his pillow–
In a utopia he will–
Never attest – the man now will–
Always cherish his boyhood ways–
As like children in a fit of glee–
Will hesitate to rest.

It seems that the well–
Of being human brings–
Storm clouds from the past–
To the surface as the beavers–
Of consciousness build–
Their dam of the good things–
In life to battle what went–
On before but darkness–
Has to be dealt with–
Before there can be light–
As a piece of drift wood–
Floats down the trickling–
Of the stream–
To gather the grandeur–
Of a traveling thought.

Submerging in a–
Thin line of blue–
Water so cool–
Becoming revitalized–
True and true–
While the bushy trees–
Off the shore of–
The pond seems–
To beckon to venture–
Closer before the–
Illusion of immortality–
Takes hold–
Safety possessing–
Its own limits–
Of constraint–
While a nonchalant duck–
Paddles by leaving–
His regards in the wake–
A single tail feather–
Floating by.

Flash flood–
The outpouring of–
Nocturnal visions unleashed–
From the breaking of the dam–
Of consciousness–
While some dreams–
Dissolve into the sentiments–
Down below while others–
Fragment to become–
An epiphany–
Of meanings not captured–
In the undertow–
With dealings of the past–
Builds one stronger–
As a whole–
A toy boat floating–
In a temporary puddle–
Only skimming the–
Surface for that–
Moment.

The forming clouds make–
A blur in the grey sky–
Such stirs the time–
To recollect friends–
Gone by as the years–
Unfold distance with–
Broken ties–
One letter my dad–
Wrote when his–
Eldest son was–
At summer camp–
The only one he–
Ever wrote was–
A cherished item–
Now lost with–
The head of the family–
Occupying an apartment–
In heaven somewhere–
Perished from this earth too–
Shows how precious–
Our moments are–
With others–
Like a tattered life boat–
Against an ocean–
of swirling rationed out todays.

The chameleon–
Blending many colors–
With the passing of gain–
Adjusts to his territory–
While our suspenders snap–
With pain–
When attempting–
To accept things–
Beyond the window pane–
The world spinning–
In a galaxy mostly–
Beyond our view–
Holds understanding–
Like a tea cup–
To sip with–
Gratitude for all–
It bestows as if–
It was nectar to–
A diligent bee–
In the mechanism–
Of life so difficult–
To swallow as a whole–
Beyond our control.

The pollen frolicked in the air–
White dandelions brushed back–
Their sunburnt hair–
Crickets chirped while–
Pretending to be invisible–
To all of us who were there–
Meandering in an old place–
A graveyard that posted–
Earlier dates of people–
Who thrived from–
Past times relations–
That inscribed upon–
Our souls – with hushed–
Tones held our hands–
With advice – like eternity–
Passing notes as if in–
Grade school while–
The teacher was at–
The chalkboard scribbling–
Lessons of life on–
A table rasa chalkboard–
Ancestors speaking beyond–
The grave – mental pictures–
To be had – staying after class–
For those who couldn't see.

Truths like legends–
Always seem to be under foot–
Leaving impressions like–
Fossils discovered–
Exposing tales without–
Spoken word said–
The stillness before–
An impending storm–
Messages released–
Before realization–
Bears witness upon–
An orphaned thought–
Before we claim it–
As our own–
Learning lessons–
Through the kaleidoscope–
Of time–
The emergence–
Of a dream–
Lends understanding–
To the whole–
Before we scatter from the rain.

Sweat trickling down–
On an afternoon stroll–
Humidity weeping out–
Of control–
Shade dished out–
From an outside canopy–
Or few – offer solitude–
Of reflections like from–
A wishing pool–
Each coin tossed–
Causes ripples of–
Hopes sinking down deep–
Their shiny coats–
Meeting the morning light–
A whistle waking–
The most focused reverie–
Stirs momentum for–
Action rather than sleep–
A leaf puffing full–
On a spring tree–
Becomes part of–
The chorus where–
The fowl perform–
For free.

The rapture of waking up–
Again brings a new perspective–
On the strings of an old day–
In gratitude of being able–
To start over again–
Interacting with nature–
And other people–
Like capturing conversations–
In a glass jar as if they–
Were lightning bugs–
Shining forth in–
Their bright ways–
Trying to wield off–
Senseless fights–
While the moment–
Parades forth–
To gather like bee–
To the pollen–
Instead of wasting–
The time like–
An overdue library book.

The ancient huge tree–
With gnarled roots sinking–
Deep in the encompassing soil–
Is much like an old man–
With each wrinkle on–
His face representing–
Years of stories like–
Untold medals from–
Serene times to–
The darkest pits–
Of despair–
All of us have–
Histories to share–
Listening to the–
Messages beyond–
The swishing of the boughs–
And the value of–
What others share–
For free–
A penny for–
Those thoughts–
Would make us rich–
Beyond the wildest–
Of our imaginations–
Could ever be.

Even in rest–
The mind never ceases–
Beyond the easy visions–
Of bees nursing the petals–
In a crowded field–
Some of the timothy stalks–
Are bent with–
Their gaze shifting down–
While the reflecting pool–
Reveals images of–
Troubling sights–
Climbing out of an abyss–
Of fears and confusion–
Soon vanishing like–
Dew glistening in–
An intricate spider web–
While the heat of the day–
Hides those somber thoughts–
That so quickly vanished away–
Until sleep beckons forth–
A new parade to–
Encounter along life's path–
Heralding in both–
The darkness and the light.

The crystal storm–
Swallowed up the town–
In early morning but–
The afternoon brought–
Melting from the warmth–
Of march where most–
Leprechauns are busy–
Polishing their coins–
In their pots of gold–
As the skunks in their–
Black and white tuxedos–
Scatter around the land–
For scraps of food–
While the world tilts–
In timely rotations–
While another day–
Unfolds like a newspaper–
Ushering in more events–
In our lives like a film–
Showing coming attractions–
Before yesterdays are–
Embalmed in memories once again.

Lazy sunny June day–
A man with his own pain–
Attempts to transcend–
The moment–
In comic relief–
He brings others–
The gift of laughter–
Rising from their throats–
Like balloons mushrooming–
To the sky–
Time seems to relish–
In its own growth–
While some trapped–
In private misery–
Never expand to–
The birth of a smile–
Only quietly always–
Walking away from it.

The boughs frolicked–
After a late march storm–
Releasing a deep breath–
While mounds of crystal flakes–
Still settled in a Vermont town–
Like guard dogs left in–
The thawing wake–
As another season–
Released her flowered hair–
Our existence always a mystery–
Where the encounters of life–
Will unfold like a gas station map–
Of destinations yet unsaid–
The bell on the tall building–
Toll even hour while–
We are awake or drifting–
Through slumber in a dream–
That echo through our–
Memory chambers–
Never explained on–
A rational plane but–
Always whispered to–
Our souls–
A budding leaf–
Proud in her vitality dress.

The chirping of–
A solitary bird on–
A cool February day–
Announcing a warbled tune–
In flight that fills–
The cobalt blue skies–
From such a fragile creature–
Bringing simple melodies–
To light in a cloud filled sky–
For a moment–
To revel in our–
Existence to witness–
Nature at her best–
While the boughs–
Wave back and forth–
Paying homage–
Of the miracle–
Of us being there.

Just a bouquet of flowers–
Fragile like you–
Soaking up water–
In a vase reflecting–
The rest of the room–
Shadows of yesterday–
Attempt to vanish–
From the cascade–
Of light beaming–
From the coffee table lamp–
Their memories etched–
Deeper than the–
Fickleness of marauders–
Of bands of dust–
Nimbly dancing into–
The history of our beings–
Before any meaning–
Can be ascribed to–
How the world–
Changes how we see–
The road we travel–
Today and an arsenal–
Of the past–
One more bud opening up.

The little boy surrounded–
By a small New Hampshire town–
Nursed dreams like–
Wet foaming bubbles–
Rising to the balconies–
Of the sky–
His domain included–
Tall grass on railroad tracks–
Where the iron horse–
Perished years before–
The child came forth–
Into this world–
Now donning the–
Face of compassion–
With laughter soothes–
The babbling of the soul–
As the fog collects–
Past the tree lines–
Of Vermont as people–
Busy with their lives–
Hesitate now and then–
To test the cool waters–
Of the mind to share–
What is really inside.

The sky holds a crowd–
Of vaporous faces–
Possessing chameleon-like–
Way of change–
While we do our best–
To adapt to a universe–
Of realities that are–
Beyond our control–
The child is by nature–
A curious soul–
While age molds us–
In our own ways–
Sampling the art–
Of youth at times–
Can be so vital–
For our perspectives–
As if peering out–
Of an open window–
In a tall cathedral–
Something new–
Always emerges–
To ponder on.

In view of a small place–
Growing up with only–
French Canadian and Polish descent–
The world held a narrow lens–
Until the navy opened up–
Many other cultures–
With an opportunity to see–
So many ways to think–
The only thing that–
Really matters is–
What comes from the heart–
If it only speaks in–
A whisper–
In the company–
Of compassion–
The boughs still–
Sound off in color–
Even when the–
Leaves shroud themselves–
In brown–
The wonder of splendor–
Has no bounds–
Or shackles on the mind to be.

Antiquity – seems like–
We capture that–
Whether we want to or not–
Youth acknowledge our throne–
Polish it – wipe the dust–
Off the shelf–
Although our younger selves–
Sings louder than–
The fowl chirping–
Among the autumn boughs–
Introducing themselves–
On chariots in our dreams–
Extending the personal–
Chapters of our books–
To all who listen–
In the syllables of–
A hush like–
A baby in his cradle–
Nursing visions being–
Invented in a slow motion–
Rush like pussy willows–
Welcoming the morning's haze.

A scattering of leaves–
Much like the ashes of others–
Like an older sister who–
Held firm the belief–
To comfort family members–
In their time of need–
We attempt to stay humble–
To relinquish from the heart–
All that we can–
Like the braiding of–
A young girl's silken hair–
An artwork of beauty–
To admire–
A scattering of leaves–
Travels of many destinations–
Laying witness to–
Many others who need–
Someone to care–
As the pumpkins–
Gather their frost–
Turned hair–
We must share–
What we bestow–
From the heart–
Before our ashes are lost.

The cool green nights–
Will soon transform–
To the bright colors–
Of the boughs–
As the fowl prepare–
To migrate–
Whole flocks of geese–
Resonate above–
Silent rooftops–
Leaving their shadows–
In their wake–
While we are left–
With the fleeting–
Warm days–
To relish like life–
While we can–
Like a discarded thought–
Left along the way.

The cuckoo clock tolled–
Every half hour and hour–
At my uncle and aunt's house–
Sleeping over there–
As a child forever kissed
By their black long haired–
Dog, Lucky–
It seems now–
That the introduction–
To the little wooden bird–
From those swinging doors–
Reminding us of moments gone–
As a boy growing up–
In a sleepy New Hampshire town–
While a greater realm–
Awaiting us beyond–
The scope of what–
We thought it–
Might be–
With each turn and twist–
Of the Merrimack River–
Could reveal —
Only silent rocks–
In a tiny shallow sea.

Soft hush like–
Velvet lined shoes–
Floating on carpet–
Broken friendships–
Always leave a scar–
Of memories tiptoeing–
Through memories–
Never fully discarded–
On to a scattered–
Floor of debris–
Reviewing an old picture–
Of the two of us together–
From years ago–
Refreshing one of–
The good times like–
A glass of cold water–
From a roaring of–
A fresh spring brook–
Always tames the–
Broken beast–
Going down.

The old man of the mountain–
Stumbled on his–
Black stony knees–
Retired in eternity–
No longer the–
Silent sentry on–
New Hampshire land–
Years of stories–
Cradled in his tomb–
A giant eagle–
Floats above his–
Solemn grave in–
Search of food–
For her newborn.

A wreath rested–
Upon the shroud–
A solemn marker–
For spectators of–
What idly presented–
Its true colors in–
The past–
Wild violets still–
Cry their names–
After perishing in–
The mowed grass–
Accomplishments that–
Have been achieved–
Need to multiply like–
Rampant rabbits–
Before any–
Ticker tape parade–
Each float more grandiose–
Than the last–
What is learned–
Begins from inside–
Mistakes solemnly–
Shake their heads–
Before trudging away.

My girlfriend whispered–
Memories of you–
Like wandering streams–
Pulsating over hidden surfaces–
In the cool undivided waters–
Of past histories–
How you could be–
Both stern when needed be–
But kindness always intervened–
Being a teacher to you–
Instructing how to cook–
While the aromas of–
What was created–
Floated through the house–
Like winged angels–
Always there for–
Her daughter even–
When your physical entity–
Vanished from our world–
As we know it to be–
Flowers from the heart–
Forever in bloom for you–
Tears of memories.

Tribute to Roslyn–

Messages from the head–
Emerging from the cloudy haze–
In nocturnal bliss–
Clear vision of a father–
Wandering on ahead–
Now almost thirty years gone–
With an attempt to call him–
Forgetting his phone number–
Dialing my mom for–
The number instead–
Only static on the line–
Phantoms prance around–
From messages from–
My head–
He waves to me–
From the porch–
In white T-shirt–
And work pants in–
Time vanished years ago–
In residence now–
In my head.

1

Hoisting up a breath–
In nocturnal rest–
Night time in a vision–
Grasshoppers hiding in the tall grass–
Becoming a colony of sound–
Beyond our grasp–
Like attempting to corner–
A lingering thought–
Like the insect–
It suddenly flies away–
Until sheer determination–
We rise beyond the contest–
To win the dream–
The lone thought–
Pondering to its self–
Transforms to a larger whole–
Extending our reality–
For the better part–
Of who we are–
Of what we are now–
Dusk's shy demeanor–
Bows down to the–
Aftermath of yesterdays.

2

Early September in Vermont–
Indian summer raising the–
Torrid heat in the stillness–
Of the air–
Hopes muster forth–
Like a company of straw hats–
Creating their own coolness–
From the sun's watchful eye–
While people saunter by–
Laden with their own agendas–
All their own even though–
They aren't inscribed in stone–
Occasionally an unexpected turn–
Can divide even the most–
Strong-willed mind–
With a new decision–
Coming forth like–
An unbridled bride.

Like a wounded robin–
I dust you off – smooth out your wings–
In hopes you will fly again without little help–
Offering my nurturing basket of love–
Upon your after of need – my presence–
Is always there for you–
Every twinge of independence–
My applause echoes through my heart–
Vibrating through the aisles–
Of my mind-that you will gather–
Strength and health together–
Like celestial twins being–
Born again.

Tribute to Roslyn–

Childhood – old sneakers worn–
Over and over again – yellow slickers–
On rainy days pregnant with–
Dark clouds rumbling like–
Empty stomachs lurching forward–
Ensuing sunshine highlighting–
Mammoth puddles housing–
Reflections of things to be–
A boy transforming through time–
No avenue to stop the change–
Like a teeter totter going up and down–
Depending on where life–
Was taking him.

Healthy plants green–
With jubilation–
Dripping newness–
From my uncle's garden – clean rows–
Of tilled soft soil from–
The sun's caress – he lumbering down–
The dirt path to our house–
Laden with paper bag full–
Of ripe red tomatoes and huge cucumbers–
For our table – a unison of family–
unspoken love – at our gathering–
On a warm summer's day–
A season blinking a blurred eye.

Too much fertilizer on–
The weeds one would suppose–
In a garden tangled by–
By gone mistakes created–
By a man with a rusty spade–
No matter how deep he digs–
The cut worms sever his–
Link to the sun and warmth above–
Sons that would be the picked prize–
Wither in the wind from–
The storms that gathered–
In a cacophony deep within–
Like a hunchback bent forth–
With the weight of the rope–
Coiled around his wrist–
To ring and ring again–
Cries bouncing off–
Silent towers with–
No inhabitants within.

Two empty park benches–
Nestled staggering grass–
Waking up from the–
A cold season–
Birds grumbling–
For a run-away crumb–
People buckled down–
In their own individual–
Realms in search–
Of lost souls–
While the Russian bear–
Wears death as a badge–
Of power while death–
Wields its bloody path–
The world spinning–
On a crooked axis–
Once more.

The preamble of a bud–
Being a renegade to–
The late march air–
Such softness in–
The harshness of–
A lingering season–
Boasting her green gown–
Harboring no chill–
But a need to be there–
The transition of mother nature–
And her off spring–
Vitality combing back–
Sleek spring hair–
Rebirth – calm and deliberate–
No creaking rocking chairs–
To disturb what will–
Soon be there.

That space above my father's garage–
Two small rooms from a rickety ladder–
And trap door to gain entrance–
My cousin and I gained a bubble–
From the madness of the world–
In this small space among the–
Rolling grassy banks of the–
Family home – peeking through–
The looking glass of a tiny window–
Of adolescence along its merry way–
While secrets held steadfast–
In cousins' resolve–
To keep bonds strong–
Among a utopia gone astray–
From a boy's jacket recovered–
From the Merrimack River–
Full of leeches–
Simply didn't belong–
The gurgling of the current–
Went steadily along.

February crystal fall–
Paints the sky white–
Walking shadows like me–
Become a mere audience–
That leaves us spell-bound–
With each intricate pattern–
Nimbly lighting down–
Cold fragile feet claiming–
The barren ground–
That hesitantly part–
With only a fleeting memory–
That it was ever found–
A crowd from up above–
Soon erased like–
A school boy cleansing–
The day's work from–
The chalk board.

She uncoiled her pointed leaves–
Across the late summer afternoon grass–
Somber yellow flowers closing–
Their fragrant petals like–
Hands in a reverent prayer–
Soon the transformation–
Would commence into–
Gourd babies growing into–
Deep orange adults clinging–
On their cloistered vines–
In anticipation of being picked.

The season soon will–
Witness the leaves burning–
In an explosion of bright colors–
In the boughs as thoughts–
Wander down vacant lots
Sensing you near feels–
Like a comforter snug around me–
In compassion and reverie–
Such a tribute is complete–
Like love folding down the sheets.

The child in his innocence–
Displayed gratitude in the–
Simple things we long forgot–
To see – like a ship lost at sea–
To finally discover a port–
Before running aground–
Like violets in the spring–
Rising up with their blueish faces–
Brings bundles of warmth–
Not only from the stroking–
Of the sun's caress but–
From people who introduce–
Themselves to their inner best–
Like you and me–
Lesson learned-don't put–
Blinders on the mind but–
Be true to the self–
That many leave behind.

Shuddering bullied young–
Hunkered down in disbelief
With adolescents found–
Their strength in breaking down–
An innocence left in the debris–
Of disbelief – years later–
Discovering self-esteem–
Among the wreckage still–
Smoldering from memories–
Never able to lay to rest–
A grave yard with many bones–
Not crumpling from ignorance–
Under uncovering the inner being–
With virtues no one could attest–
The landscape so full–
Of inner protest.

The ageless librarian–
Dusted off the shelves–
Of categories that–
Curious minds succumbed to–
Each selection – exposing their–
Taunt bindings to the mind–
Every flavor of thought–
Unleased hordes of–
The imagination weakening–
The borders of simplicity–
Of the expectations of–
What should be succeeded–
For the rational of the–
Beginning of the birth–
Of the mother in–
The rocking chair–
With soothing words–
Of what is right–
Each creak of the chair–
Vibrating questions–
Of an understanding–
Of truths hidden–
From sight.

Scrambling up on the roof–
Inching up the stone wall–
Unfinished open garage that–
Set against the rolling back–
Lawn bank with drooping–
Willow tree like a sad Medusa–
With fatten leaves – felt like–
King of the hill on top of the world–
After a day of bullying from–
The elementary school broke–
My spirit like a hellion horse–
Reined in after running free–
A wide view across willow hill–
To my buddy's family store–
Until the pink and blue–
Of dusk clenched hands–
As the grey performed–
Its surrender to the night–
As dad walked out on porch–
Telling me it was time to–
Come in for the day–
Hope grew in the clatter–
Of notes against a page–
Of agenda for the next moment–
That held possibilities of hope yet banished.

There was a youth/man–
In my youth on the beach–
Of graveled pebbles in–
My home town–
He was from Canadian/French–
Descent who liked to sing–
Happy melodies–
Norman always said with–
His thick French accent–
"who thing better"–
The children would make fun–
Of him – taunting him relentlessly–
But this child always responded–
"You sing better, Norman"–
"You sing better"–
Such cruelty should–
Be marooned on–
A deserted island far away–
While his songs wafted idly–
Through time and the–
Summer breeze everywhere.

This November day so–
Blustery blue – eased my mind–
Searching for: revelations–
Swirling in the exhalation–
Of a lazy gust of wind–
Of the tail end of–
Conversations deep within–
From a child floating on a row boat–
Beyond the din with–
Uncle Rudy to visiting–
A fish hatchery with him–
Stoking the wonder of–
The heart leaving embers–
Never to completely–
Be extinguished with–
Only other memories–
Casting it back to–
A roaring fire blazing bright–
With shadow puppets–
Prancing all about–
With no admission needed–
Just to sit back to enjoy–
The show again.

Morning rose erasing–
Its half-awake eyes–
From the titillating way–
The dormant leaves–
Swam in from their–
Midnight bath while–
The grey fog unraveled–
Upon Brattleboro town–
Paralleling the haze–
Bestowed from the mind–
Released from the throes–
Of slumber as the shadows–
Of the landscape grew–
Sharper as thoughts–
Chattered as if they–
Were children frolicking–
On an inviting playground–
For the first time–
A grandeur scheme–
Of life while the–
School bells chimed–
Their cadence that–
Memory had claimed–
Another moment for ransom again.

Huddled up to the–
Frigid air – donning–
The observer's hat–
As November took–
Over the reigning crown–
The park benches lay bare–
The cacophony of voices–
Thinned from the crowd–
A stubborn leaf–
Finally tumbled down–
Like a toddler on–
The first step–
Clear blue skies–
Brightened my reverie–
Phantoms of thought–
Whirled about like–
A washing machine–
Chuckling to spin–
Gathering them all up–
Like wandering sheep–
To regain the meaning–
Of the whole–
With the beginning of the cold.

Autumn rain drops blush–
As they serenade the ground–
In their wept full surprise–
Through the half-naked trees–
From the grey clouded sky–
A few birds chirp–
With their dismay–
That the brightness of the sun–
Will soon creep forward–
To fill the day–
Leaving puddles as–
Reflecting pools for–
Everyone's gaze.

The leaves in–
Perfect patterns–
Afford the ground–
In their crisp maze–
Crunching down on–
Their brittle bones–
Breaks the silence–
In the pre-dawn day–
Like the mystery–
Of the dinosaurs–
In another era–
Some time before–
The birth of tomorrow–
Full of yesterdays.

Disgruntled on the beaten path–
So many injustices crowding–
The streets – a beggar asking–
For money to fill his pockets–
Only to artificially expand his mind–
In Brattleboro, Vermont–
Where the foliage briefly–
Dresses the boughs–
To be strip naked with–
The season's demise–
No simple answers can–
Complete the tangled web–
Of the ones who wander–
In defeat-on hilly roadside–
Tents torn and scattered–
Populate the town–
A humble vagabond–
Strums a guitar against–
A down town building's side–
With hopes of a few dollars–
Will be tossed in his music case–
Makes my fortunes seem–
So vast like the discovery–
Of a leprechaun's pot to face.

Heavy laden with–
The crystal-clear revelation–
Of the moment like–
A magician's sleight of hand–
So many facets give warmth–
To the turbulence of the day–
Acknowledging people in–
Their vast array no matter–
How far they stray from–
The herds of my beliefs–
Garnishes one with–
Confidence especially within–
Troubled waters like–
A buoyant canoe upon–
Pleasant lake–
Harmony with a life jacket–
Floating peacefully on–
Tamed surfaces in–
The thickest of marsh–
For every breathing creature–
Becomes our existence–
Beyond any one's control–
Finding something positive —
Along the way.

Met with some friends–
For a social rendezvous–
But was cast in a superficial–
Diffused light of conversations–
That didn't quench my–
Intellectual yearnings–
Like gulping water–
From inexhaustible thirst–
In an empty cup–
Attempting to broaden–
Connections of people–
Who can satisfy these needs–
In rural Brattleboro–
To bring more life to me–
Much as Frankenstein–
Did to the monster–
With each zap of the–
Lightning bolt–
Vitality born again–
From a cerebral womb–
Words strung together–
Like presents left under–
The Christmas tree for me.

Mid-October in Vermont–
The geese signal from overhead–
In wing formation they chant–
A guttural farewell for now–
Against a grey blue sky–
Sitting in my porch chair–
Wading through the annuals–
Of life so far that has taken me–
To many pinnacles and abysses–
Hearing the fowls' sad adieu–
As the boughs still hold–
Their green parlor soon–
To burst into colors–
Like a prism reflecting–
The spectrum of light–
Each moment out on–
Those blustery days–
Gathering something simple–
As a passing smile–
Creates the imagination–
In my mind to feel the good–
Like children dancing–
In a circle – innocence revisited–
For a split second in time–
Contentment with the coming of night.

Jubilation – a celebration of self–
Watching the leaves in their seasonal twitch–
To soon become emblazon in–
Portraits of fiery change–
Makes me so content to walk the streets–
With each step a possibility of an encounter–
With another person with a story–
To exchange among the crisp autumn air–
Building upon what came before–
The book so full but not without
An excerpt or two not included in–
The final product of great faith–
Transformed into a filter of–
What I see – taking the good–
And the bad – my character stands strong–
Amid the flutter of a falling leave–
Of a season to believe–
That Halloween with a myriad of masks–
To soon take off–
To show what lies beneath–
The surface to believe–
The cacophony of laughter–
Of children full of treats.

The boughs tickled by–
The whispery wind–
Anticipated their children–
To quickly turn colors depending on–
The seasons' folly from warm afternoons–
To chill added to the air–
Limbs ablaze in golds, orange and reds–
Woke up the deadened debris–
Of the memories caught in–
A boy's mind–
The trees so alive–
Whispering their messages–
From days gone by–
With the flutter of a dying flower–
To the cocoons closing tight–
To a sleep of transformation–
Like beauty and the beast–
Dancing to the midnight hour–
Before change over powered–
What ultimately had to be right–
A butterfly would be soaring later–
In a field reawakening in another season–
Soon to be.

Dowry for a pleasant fall day–
People scattered on the sidewalk–
Adrift in their own conversations
Dogs hungrily looking on–
At their masters for a treat–
Or simple pat on the head–
Clouds evolving in–
Fleecy characters of–
Drifting faces colliding–
Into themselves to form–
Into another like a chameleon–
Changing fate – just an observer–
Stepping on – in rural Vermont–
The warmth of hope–
Like a charm bracelet rattles on–
Each time spent in grace–
Of wisdom burning bright–
In the darkest of nights–
Where no thoughts go–
Unturned as if they were–
Like a pauper's grave–
Exhumed for the truths–
That lay exposed beyond.

Early autumn–
The boughs prancing–
In new hairdos – while the wind–
Ruffled up the children of tree color–
Life so alive on a warm September day–
Before the chill of another season–
Crept through the rafters–
In the second of a moment–
Of a random blur of time–
When the grandeur of the moment–
Crept like catlike stealth near–
The table of the present–
Like fine silverware–
To dine–
No waiter to pick up–
The check – where the–
Tips are rationed to–
The divine.

Following the crowd–
In college – a feeling made–
Me depart on my own–
Every Friday – to choose the path–
To take – devoid of any consensus vote–
Springing from an eruption of whim–
Discovering the mother vein–
Of satisfaction from–
Where to choose a journey–
That my own inner architect–
Drew the blueprints of a world–
Unknown but exciting–
Like a dinosaur exploring–
A virgin forest —
Before extinction–
Was ultimately engraved on–
Any living thing.

Phantoms of yesterday–
Crisp autumn leaves of childhood–
Thrashing through hordes of their–
Crinkle and crunch while the–
Sun beamed along the path–
The gigantic church clock–
In west franklin pushing–
Its arm resting on another moment in time–
Whispered me nothing in–
An innocence of past days–
What tomorrow could bring–
From a sleepy town resting–
On its secrets of ancestors–
Laying in eternity–
Only tombstones protruding–
Their granite heads in–
Salute of tomorrows —
Yet to be.

In accordance–
With my membrane of life–
Skeletons rattle in their cages–
Still vibrate their own tales today–
Their puzzles a query to sit down–
At the haphazard card table to–
Figure out where the missing pieces–
Might fit – the whole being just–
An illusion to be introduced someday–
When the finality like–
A clown's curtsey is met–
The grease paint weathered loose–
Revealing everything underneath–
The curtain rising once last time–
To an audience of one or many–
Who knows what to think–
A rattle of an empty tin can–
From a boy kicked across the street.

Autopsy of a moment–
Bares its cerebral instruments–
With surgical gloves–
In dissecting frenzy–
Exposing the raw virtues underneath–
A caliber of person–
Deep within ego's catacomb–
Wrestles with his eternity–
Like a kitten chasing–
A ball of–
Yarn–
Unraveling as time–
Pursues close behind–
As the present evaporates–
Like the fog of an early morning sun.

Leaves now–
In their brown shrouds–
Mask the ground before–
A sheet of white covers–
Up their peaceful slumber–
A wisp now and there–
Of crystal bandits–
Lightly tumble down–
Like scouts before–
The whole sky–
Turns white confusing–
Perceptions huddled down–
Like a movie screen with–
A blank slate until–
The next feature–
Comes to life.

A sleepy turtle–
Covered by the shadow–
Of his shell–
Limits his existence–
From the world as–
The confusion of–
A world defies logic–
In a realm of interruption–
Sounding from the–
Tranquility caressing–
A little boy's head–
That the moment now–
Can be good–
Only the mismatch–
Of perception of the–
Strangulation of the–
Underbrush hides the–
Brilliance of the mind–
That the passing of–
The truth can hold–
Its wings and soar–
Above the debris–
Of the congealed thought–
Look to the skies–
For the answers so sublime.

The sentiments of–
A grasshopper always–
On alert – swaying with–
The dancing grass–
Maybe if we could–
Grab some of the flexibility–
A tiny insect exudes forth–
In its kingdom of the land–
To capture a minute that–
Transpired–
Before past visions–
Gained control–
To trap a time–
Before it is long gone–
A flinching tree–
Signals its dismay
An acorn spewed–
From the fragile bough–
A Hercules of a future–
Climbs forth.

Face plastered against–
The crystal ball–
With dome shining–
For one and all–
From the window pane–
Glimmering like dew–
Tearing on the morning lawn–
In what could be–
Snowy flakes in the globe–
When turned upside down–
Still reveal the same scene–
The formation of–
Tomorrows never–
Shed any light–
Like a sleepy maiden–
Woken from a dream–
A cerebral ship–
Aground at night–
Never drifts off–
Where the sand holds tight–
Only murmuring beneath–
The ocean's heartbeat–
Whispering half-truths–
In the evening's air–
A seagull darts forth with a crumb–
Held hostage in its beak.

Some words lay like–
A lioness on the prowl–
Lashing out in disregard–
To devour innocence–
Of ideas from others–
Like an unsuspecting guest–
Hiding in the tall grass–
Not for survival–
Be as it may–
Just for the hunger–
To dominate–
To abandon others'–
Dreams within the–
Structure of a of hollow cave–
Where the darkness–
Doesn't hail from the eyes–
But through the heart–
From where it came–
The bones of existence–
Need not a name.

Sheets pinned across–
The clothes line thrashed–
Seemingly to be released–
And prevail–
Their shadows prancing–
Against the sunlit lawn–
Tales of childhood–
Clipped with the–
Surrender of simpler ways–
Magically escaped as–
If the pins holding–
The garments consented–
To the wind like–
Visions of the past–
Became chapters in history–
Spirits trying so earnestly–
To float away–
To reappear some–
Other way–
Chimes shouting–
In melodies of–
Applause.

Tantamount–
History breathes–
My tale within–
Hiccups of disbelief
Of flaws within–
The cage of–
Trudging forward–
Without a manual–
To always prove–
The best in judgement–
To dispel relief–
Grasping at the–
Better pieces of the maze–
Creates a vision–
That is difficult to–
Not stare at–
Such positive ways–
Born from the womb–
Could hide such–
Shadows along the way–
Hopefully a student–
In the classroom of life–
Always raising his hand–
To ask questions along the way.

Turbulence – the whisk of–
A budding flower–
Petal unveiling–
A fragility at the core–
Show casing the awards–
Within the case–
You are the warm stalk–
Radiating the warmth–
Without rays of the sun–
To feel the vibrations–
Instilled in you–
A man attempting–
To compliment you–
Sometimes falls–
Within his flaws–
Always returning to–
His feet to bestow–
Satisfaction at its best–
His heart pounding–
To be with you–
A saved rose–
Enveloped in a book.

Tribute to Roslyn

The babies of–
Thoughts lumbering–
Misdirected from the past–
Cry, laugh, and whimper–
For validation from–
Our inner self–
Dozing under the–
Family's willow tree–
Trying to understand–
The past and where–
It belonged–
People in our lives–
Float upon a song–
The lyrics coming–
And going without–
A sound–
A shadow rifling–
Through things discarded–
From the past–
With unknowingly–
Treasures in their–
Shaking hands.

Comforter snug tight–
Doesn't warm the mind–
In its habitat of visions–
Whirling in a dervish–
Of messages caught–
Behind the haze–
Of questions from–
Yonder plains of youth–
To adulthood reminiscing–
Days long played–
Once the leader of–
A few friends who–
Depended what the agenda–
Was for that time–
So much burden for–
The youngest of the pack–
To make if it was for–
The best or just ill gain–
A soft-spoken pal–
Kept his bees–
Singing their songs in–
His mother's backyard–
Seemed so simple–
In their reign.